Petty Theft

Petty Theft

POEMS

Nicholas Friedman

WINNER OF THE NEW CRITERION POETRY PRIZE

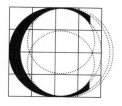

Criterion Books
NEW YORK

*Funding for this year's New Criterion Poetry Prize
has been provided by Joy & Michael Millette*

First American edition published in 2018 by Criterion Books, an imprint
of Encounter Books, an activity of Encounter for Culture and Education,
Inc., a nonprofit, tax-exempt corporation.
www.newcriterion.com/poetryprize

Library of Congress Cataloging-in-Publication Data

Names: Friedman, Nicholas, author.
Title: Petty theft : poems / Nicholas Friedman.
Description: New York : Criterion Books, 2018.
Identifiers: LCCN 2018041309 | ISBN 9781641770224 (hardcover : alk. paper)
Classification: LCC PS3606.R567 A6 2019 | DDC 811/.6–dc23
LC record available at https://lccn.loc.gov/2018041309

for my family

Contents

III

IV

Petty Theft

I have heard it said that rats collect trinkets, that if you expose a rat's nest, you may find bright bits of glass and other small desirable objects.

—E. B. White

I

The Magic Trick

Half clown, half Keebler elf, he works a throng
of meth heads and young mothers who peruse
the storefronts, tugging surly kids along.
The pant legs bunch around his wingtip shoes.

When a couple walks up to his TV tray,
he hands them each a tattered business card.
"Who wants to see a magic trick today?"
He mugs and cuts a deck. His hands are scarred

but seldom shake. The two confer, agree,
and fidget as the magician fans an arc
of cherubs laced with flips of filigree.
The man inspects them for a telltale mark,

but they look clean. I've watched him do this trick
for weeks now, each time to polite surprise:
He hams it up, he lays the charm on thick;
as always, haughty jacks materialize.

The woman smiles and nods, as if content.
Another trick: He pulls a wrinkled bill
from his lapel and folds the president,
explaining how "a wise investment will

turn one buck into ten," et cetera.
He taps twice on the bill, a modest "one,"
unfolds it square by square, and then *voila!* —
the bust of Alexander Hamilton.

They clap as the magician takes a bow.
He's greasy, but he's on the up-and-up,
and magic tricks are good enough for now.
The woman floats a dollar to his cup.

Not the Song, but After

Now everywhere the pageantry of youth
    is on display:
The squeal of bike chains spinning through the gray
    plays fugue to puddle froth;

the punctual blitz of hyacinths in April
    ushers spring
with lavender, dripped from the upturned wing
    of wind-swept Gabriel.

A youngish pair walks wired at the arms—
    she casually ribbing
him, he lightly brushing her breast, jibbing
    their step to spare the worms

stranded along the road. Too soon, their laughter
    rises and goes
drifting toward silence. And now the young man knows
    love's not the song, but after—

like the mute, remembered chorus of the rain
    that stains the walk
long after falling, or the lifeless stalk
    still hoisting its head of grain.

Uneasy now, she loosens from his hand.
    Their dark familiars
stare back, reflected by the passing cars,
    with speechless reprimand.

Before the chill, each chartered hell grows hotter;
    still, every burn
will teach him how to run—and how to turn
    her wine back into water.

Undark

". . . contains real radium and will glow for years."

Not light, but darkness partially defied.
Hunched above powder and squat jars of glue,
they painted numerals on paper faces,
pointing the camel hair between their lips.
"Don't worry," their bosses said. "A little bit
of radium will give you rosy cheeks."
And so they reveled in self-luminescence,
sneezed lightning through the pitch of bedroom sky
and glowed like faint auroras in their beds.

Their jaws plumped up like ornamental gourds,
grew soft, and soon their teeth fell out like seeds.
Some blamed the paint, but others carried on
dribbling the green-white liquid through their curls
and mocking up mustaches for a laugh.
Fear only turns the key on what it knows.
One girl daubed her teeth to spook a lover
in the grin-lit dark. Now, in that other dark,
there's still a bit of light left in her bones.

—for the Radium Girls of Orange, N.J., 1917–1926

Il Poverello

at the Basilica of Saint Francis of Assisi

i. Carità

He's barefoot, wearing a handsewn burlap cloak
that rises where his back builds to a hunch.
Speaking Italian through a spittled smile,
he works the pilgrims waiting to be searched
by Carabinieri clutching their M12s.
In Rome, the gypsy children by the fountain
scattered like schools of fish when they were noticed.
But no one chases this man off. They listen,
laugh, and touch his arm. After his speech,
he offers them *libretti religiosi*,
spines barely broken, for a small donation.
He gestures with a copy as I pass.
I shake my head in plain American,
clutching my Euros, wincing at the brief
desire to tear the cloak and see his back.
The pale stone blanches under midday sun.

ii. The Transept

A sudden change of light, and then the smell
of spaded clay. A boy, pink-faced and buzzing,
bolts past me, shouting "ah!" in little blips
and listening for the echo. It's not a bad
technique, I think, though others kneel instead.

He grabs the velvet rope that leads us in,
jostles it—"ah!"—and stills for the return.
Which comes, albeit from the lower nave,
star-flecked and endlessly cerulean.

iii. Sermon to the Birds

". . . *because ye know not how to spin or sew,*
  God clotheth you."

"NO PHOTO"

The trick, it seems, was getting them to listen—
to keep a single, coalescent style.
But *Giotto's own hand*, rather than his school's,
is quite apparent here. A dove, now faded,
drifts down from a pompom tree to join
the flock. I check the guidebook. Beautiful.
A second friar watches, rapt as we are
by their looking on, and by the way
they gather and appear to understand.
And open up their beaks, as if to pray.

iv. In the Crypt

A restless train of pilgrims shoulder up
to where, beyond the rows of moving lips,
a hewn stone pillar wrapped with iron ties
contains the bones, apparently intact.

It's mostly candles and a crucifix,
some marble and an s. FRANCESCO plaque.
OFFERTA seems like more than a suggestion.
A sprawling orchid by the altar's base
bathes in the flicker of artificial light—
so much the way it was, so much made new
since *Fra Elias hid the saint from thieves* . . .
We trust that these are actually his bones.
A monk sits at a small desk, selling cards
to the bereaved. I cross myself, move forward,
and touch the pillar, darkening its stone.

The No— Pond Hermit

hadn't had human contact since Chernobyl.
Or, rather, once he squeaked a startled "hi"
to quell suspicion from a passer-by.
His hard-won solitude has now gone global

thanks to a spread in *GQ Magazine*,
but once he was the undisputed lord
of all he kept, and all that buoyed or bored
him on the daily. Work never came to lean

against his days; Monday was just a thought
that joined the welter in the minds of others.
Of course, there *were* inevitable bothers:
to steal, well, *everything*; to not get caught;

to not light fires for fear of that. To live.
Funny to think that his foremost ambition
was dodging what we'd die for: recognition,
as if life's crowning purpose were to give

biographers a steady lead to follow.
J. Salzman was, for thirty years, the dean
of Arts and Sciences. He reached the mean
income in record time. His vague and hollow—

et cetera. Folks long presumed him dead,
but hidden cameras caught him pilfering
coffee, Smarties, and hamburger last spring—
all from a campground dining hall, the spread

explains. Now, he awaits a public trial—
and judgment by a jury of his peers.
His hopes and fears are not our hopes and fears.
His glasses are three decades out of style.

The Outlaws of Missouri, 1883

They take the stage in Abilene, road-tired
and a little high. A year back, Bob became
the man who shot The Outlaw Jesse James;
now he's the man who shoots his sickly brother,
over and over, for a modest fee.
Charley hacks into his handkerchief
and mounts the chair the way he did in Booneville,
pretending to right a crooked needlepoint.
Some of the crowd shows up to heckle Bob.
A man shouts "Judas" as the hammer cocks
on his six-shot Smith & Wesson .44.
Charley wears a small obsidian pin
on his lapel, the way James did. A flash
of black glass light. A hush. A crack, and when
Bob's "bullet" catches Charley below the ear,
he falls like a gunnysack, the way he will
after pressing a revolver to his chest
in Richmond, snuffing the laudanum dropper's call,
the fevers of consumption, and the shame.
Bob will follow silver into Creede,
where he'll get neck-shot by the man who killed
the man who killed The Outlaw Jesse James.

In Flight

We suffer the cabin's choked and common air
and touch half-willingly. *For work or pleasure?*
Attendants trundle carts from nose to tail,
dispensing Coke, V8, and blackish coffee.
One with a thin gray scarf and brunette bob
reaches for cocktail napkins and a bag
of peanuts when the plane quakes suddenly
and dips us like a bobber. A light dings on.
I count the smooth blue seats, doing the math
they'll use to make a headline out of us.
An infant cries out like a tiny engine.
I've nearly hummed my way through every verse
of "Oh My Darling, Clementine" the second
we stagger into calm. Somehow I'm eating
a bag of peanuts, mouthing the ductile foil
into a silver shape, shaking them out.
The flight attendant's unchanged face stares down
from the narrow parenthetical of her hair,
saying, "Sir," and then, "*Sir*," until I realize
she's calling *me*, blinking a generous Morse
across the seats. "A whiskey, thank you. Yes."
Outside my window, thirty thousand feet
below our path, a river has bunched itself
into omegas, blinding where the sun
moves over them—while here, above all that,
the body shudders, and carries us along.

Waiting on Results

In a dark, wood-paneled studio, I've sat
for three full days, an eremite with neither
cup nor cause. As hours accumulate,

I watch my thoughts return to one conjecture:
the endgame that is neither lost nor won,
but brings itself to bear on every creature

with rules we never could quite settle on.
Instead we love, and say that it's enough,
each day approaching the meridian

which marks, invisibly, our turn from life
toward that lacuna of imagination.
We toil like pilgrims up a mortal bluff

that has no view, but is our final station.

As Is

Just north of town, a quaint Sargasso Sea
for bric-a-brac: The barn, itself antique,
spills over with a grab-bag panoply
of outworn stock revalued as "unique."
Typewriters tall as headstones fill the loft
where they've been ricked away like sacks of grain;
a coffer yawns the must of oak—gone soft—
when one man, squinting, lifts the lid to feign
intrigue. Nearby, his wife surveys the smalls:
art deco bangles brash as harpsichords,
a glut of iron trivets, Christmas balls,
Depression glass, and warping Ouija boards.
One man's junk is another's all the same.
They don't buy much, but that's not why they came.

The Vanishing Bird Cage

A parlor trick:
One white canary
rocks on a perch
until a twitch
of muscle sends
both cage and bird
disappearing
up a sleeve.
It isn't hard
to make belief
(or else the news
is magic, too).
The bigger trick
is reconciling
each with each—
the sprung device,
the bloody bird
thrown out backstage.
The act's name is
itself a willful
misdirection:
How does the cage—?
Like logic, it's
collapsible.

Petty Theft

They scattered maps and old receipts, then left
the doors pulled wide. An ersatz moon threw light
on everything they weren't looking for.
Loose change made constellations on the floor.

You shook for half the night. "No loss," I said,
cupping a breast as we each drifted off
toward half-congruent dreams or none at all,
our crooked bodies nesting at the crooks.

And that was love—the careful quietness
that kept the bed we made. And so we lay,
oblivious to the years that we'd spend aching
for what we could have missed, had it been taken.

Tiny Tina

At two-foot-five, she's queen of county fairs,
and in the ads, red velvet keeps her breasts
snugged into place like outsized Christmas pears.
Proudly ALIVE and EDUCATIONAL,
she waves a tiny greeting to her guests.
A mammoth spaniel guards the sense of scale.

Admission has been fifty cents for years.
Inside, she slouches toward a TV set,
an eight-inch black-and-white with bunny ears
whose tabloid talk show voices bleep and blare.
The interest in her eyes proves counterfeit.
Popcorn flecks the rondure of her hair.

She's stoic, squat palms resting on the paunch
that swells beneath her sundress like a buoy.
Is "Tina" real? A nervous couple hunch
to look, then startle at her perfect speech:
"My name is Gloria. I'm fifty-three . . . "
She points to photos with a Sistine reach —

her family framed above the Mason jar
that pings and clinks with fallen pocket change.
She puckers for a crowd of vinegar,
eyes fastened to the tube's half-snowed display.
Teen Mom Leaves Infant, Goes on Drinking Binge.
The picture reels toward heaven, endlessly.

Out on the midway, half-light streaks through smoke
from funnel cakes that froth in vats of grease.
The Ferris wheel flicks on, spoke after spoke.
They'll tear her cottage down at dawn, she knows,
then truck her south to find new crowds to please—
a cul-de-sac of footprints when she goes.

Titan Arum

"But *not* a flower," you say. "An inflorescence."
We blunder through the eager swarm and tack
to where its spadix thrusts up like a lighthouse
above this sea of heads. "Fine," I concede,
annoyed at toddlers piggybacked and bunching
their terrible faces. A teen mutters "crooked cock"
and walks off, laughing with his gangly crew.

Closer, we peer into the outsized funnel
of its spathe—a ribbed, unfurling ripple
in burgundy. We've come for spoiled flesh,
and as we lower nose to plant, it puffs
the stench of rodents festering in a wall.
"It's wonderful," you say, wide-eyed, unblinking,
pulsing my hand. But as the greenhouse breeds
its world inside a world, I only think
of *rot, rot, rot*, and plunge my face back in.

Compulsion

at the Texas Prison Museum, Huntsville

i.

"Before the federal government stepped in,
the inmates all did mandatory work,"
he tells me, nodding at a landscape shot
of young men turning over rocky soil.
The gift shop still sells pistol caddies, caps,
and leather Bible covers made Inside,
"but now it's all done volunteer."
                                        A sign
prohibits us from sitting in Old Sparky.
I poke my head into a mock-up cell
complete with shanks, the same as on TV.
"Now would you look at that," he says, amused.
A small display describes how inmates choose
to use their skills for either BAD or GOOD:
the cardboard armor lined with razorblades;
the Harley-Davidson carved out of wood.

ii.

A wrong turn leads us down a street that T's
at Walls—where, sure enough, brick walls square off
the prison yard. Strung up that high, barbed wire
seems almost decorative, like Christmas lights.
A white-washed school bus passes, and the guards
swivel inside their glassed-in posts.
                              "That's where
the yahoos come to protest executions,
burning their flags and whatnot on the street,"
he says, pointing a finger toward the brick.
"They'd rather see the murderers go free."
We K-turn.
                 "Well, New Zion Baptist Church
is just a few blocks down Montgomery . . . "

We pull in, order plates of chopped beef, ribs,
and slaw, then lunch on lacquered tables lined
with cut-out accolades from *Texas Monthly*.
My Dr Pepper fizzes like a wire.
"Burning the flag for evil murderers—
can you believe that? They're such *nasty* people."
He eats his plate of meat. And I eat mine.

Fever Dream

And when I startled underneath the sink,
my eyes drew open to a question mark
of knuckled pipe, its low curve asterisked
with incandescent light. Still, you were dark,

backlit, your mouth an "O" above the robe
that parted as both hands made nervous fists.
Blood on the tile; dull pain; and trumping those,
the interruption of your nakedness.

You eased me back to bed, then built a scene
from what I'd missed: the bungled piss; the fall;
the way the radiator caught my arm
and pushed the skin up like a parchment scroll.

You kept my north, a pinprick as I drifted
on waves of bed sheets stuttering out to sea.
My small craft faltered. Each time I woke, I woke
to you, who watched the rise and fall in me.

Ages ago, all that. And where did we—?
You write sometimes; I wish you well across
the interval of years. A shrinking scar
still maps that primitive geography.

TO WHOM IT MAY CONCERN, PLEASE FILL OUT THE FOLLOWING QUESTIONS AND MAIL. THIS IS A SCIENTIFIC EXPERIMENT BY DENNIS KOMSA, AGE 12.

from a note dated August 16, 1963, found sealed in a Mason jar off the Jersey Shore

The first step is to get the message lost—
though not *too* long—so its recovery
can hold significance. In this motif,
boy puts his note to sea. Hope, being brief,
dies out soon after curiosity.
And yet the jar turns up, its glass embossed

with cursive letters, somehow still intact
since floating off in 1963.
Inside, a crudely folded questionnaire
asks little more than *how* and *when* and *where*
it steered into another's custody—
in other words, the overwhelming fact

of being. The greeting toys with fate, if not
tautology: TO WHOM IT MAY CONCERN . . .
Scribbled in blue—half lower case, half caps—
the letter is a lesson in *perhaps*.
A tarnished nickel meant for the return
rattles the glass like a persistent thought.

A virtue, sure—but what will come to rile
our days? What if the good life means
steeling ourselves against the ordinary
while sussing risks out like an actuary?
Even here, the common intervenes:
In fifty years, the jar sailed half a mile.

The boy, too, never left that stretch of sea,
and so his note came back like an immense
memory never made. Now, fixed in age,
he lingers near the bottom of the page,
where one last question begs uncommon sense:
Is there anything else which might help me?

Nostos

No, you can't, but in a minor sense,
it happens every time: this half-return
past altered storefronts, houses up for sale.
The lamppost sprouting from a grassy berm
glows by the driveway where my rental car
makes the familiar turn to something strange.
The sound of one door shutting makes its point.
Inside, my bed seems someone else's bed.
I hang my wrinkled button-downs, then pull
the blinds, letting the lamplight draw its shapes
along the far white wall. Tomorrow, noise
will fill these rooms: him singing Bobby Vee
in pinched falsetto while she clatters dishes.
The way it was will turn to present tense.
We'll drink our coffee, eat, and reminisce
about the lives we hope, someday, to miss.

Rasmus Nielsen

*BLACKSMITH AND STRONGMAN OF
MOTHER LODE 1902 TO 1937, WHEN HE BEGAN
A 23-YEAR CAREER WITH BARNUM & BAILEY
CIRCUS FEATURED INTERNATIONALLY AS THE
WORLD'S STRONGEST AND MOST TATTOOED MAN.
HE LIFTED 2250 LBS.*

— Gravestone Inscription, Angels Camp

i.

I dreamed in ink—clouds pinned against the endless belly
of the sky, a blot of orange weeping through its border—
and woke to cold, damp gauze unraveling from my skin.
In time, I started drawing odd looks on the street,
so what couldn't be hidden, I forced further into view.
I figured crowds would pony up to see me inked,
like Omi and Costentenus—that self-bred lot.
Nights, after the forge was cooled, tools hung, I tracked
down Brooklyn Joe—a good man, clever with the needle—
who darkened the canvas of my flesh with dragons and geishas,
redwoods on my calves and Christ-heads on my ribs.
All told, Joe left me looking like a tall Ming vase—
a frozen scene that you could live inside for days.
My ticket elsewhere, paid in flesh. *Come look, come look.*

ii.

Those tattoos formed the hopeful specters of my night,
but morning pried me from my ink-stained sheets to work.
With crisscrossed tongs chirping like a cardinal,
I drew out horseshoes, sixteen-penny nails beside
the rictus of a forge yawning its ball of heat,
lump coke glowing and pulsing in a shallow gullet.
Working both sledge and chisel, I had no striker—preferred
to work alone. Damp leather gloves, the ceaseless ping
of hammer and anvil—these are the things I can't forget
even now, not that I hear the whisper of regret.
All that I made from broken springs, discarded chain links
rusted and thick as from the docks of Sønderborg,
are out there still. And I take comfort knowing that
somewhere a horse presses shod hooves into mud.

iii.

But curiosity's a fickle boy, and inked men
fell from wonder when the crowds thinned, wanting more:
Where Omi filed his teeth to points and stretched his lobes,
I forged a set of bull rings—four-inch, heavy gauge—
and pierced my nipples with a drawn-out, steel-grade rod,
then slid the rings into those burning tips of flesh.
Starting small, I wrapped a fifty-pound anvil in chains,
and hooking it to my chest, I lifted, slow at first,
the only sound the tick of blood against the floor.
Breath was the bitch to master—keep the good air in.
I ground my molars smooth and clenched my neck to wires.
Practice makes perfect. No, practice makes permanent.
And this, I figured, was the tempered ease of freaks—
the pearl of pain onlookers rub themselves against.

iv.

I worked the Odditorium, then joined the Ringling
sideshow's mobile hall of lesser gods and muses.
We etched our way across the country's sprawling back
and passed the whiskey till the jug got warm and greasy.
Chuffing east through Lincoln, we played Hearts and stud
as rain dragged ragged lines along the windowpanes.
Near Dallas, the giantess pulled aces on my jacks.
The towns changed faces, but the people stayed the same.
By July of 1944, a permanence:
Breasts dangled from my unseen muscle, Tiresias-like,
and the loosed-up piercings swung like cowbells when I walked.
With jagged bits of swarf still clinging to my boot soles,
I lifted for a drop-jawed crowd. You'd call it art,
if it were yours—this painting with a shifting frame.

v.

In Hartford, I woke early to a reveille
of smells—elephant shit and roughnecks boiling coffee,
day-old stuff, squatting in the long light of morning
or pissing opposite the tracks that brought us there.
Vendors trundled in their franks and orangeade,
the sunlight glinting hard against their silver carts.
Hours later came the folks who looked to patch the war
with the exotic, stuffing their faces with cotton candy,
happy as Cheshires, their little fists full of balloons.
There, children gawked as I prepared my act. One boy
screamed like a steam whistle and hid in mama's skirts.
I hooked the chain-linked anvil to my chest, then heaved,
arms spread for balance like an umpire calling *safe*.
Attraction curdled with disgust like yin and yang.

vi.

Frieda spoke politely from her leather stool,
smart in a lace-trimmed velvet dress. Some folks looked on
as if her limblessness might lead them to a sacred pity,
but she looked back more mystified than those who frowned.
Pen pressed between her chin and shoulder, Frieda signed
Best wishes on her portrait with a master's ease.
(That girl could thread a needle with just tongue and teeth.)
Looking at my hands, their knuckles fat as chestnuts,
I thought of Frieda from my platform—but it's here
that memory dims. I know "The Stars and Stripes Forever"
kicked up from the bandstand—*Allegro*, perfect, loud.
Some must have screamed; they always did. A minor hitch,
I figured—but as the band piled verse on added verse,
disaster crackled through the hope of false alarm.

vii.

We gathered outside the Big Top: There, the sad-faced clowns,
frowning as if always braced for tragedy,
grew into humans as the paint drooled off their faces.
One woman dumbly clutched an infant, charred and blebbed,
hair weeping off in wet clumps as she stroked its head.
A gust sent flames unfurling east, the band still roaring
while the canvas folded, gentle as a swan's wing lowering
on a clutch of eggs. Air heaved out like a simple sigh.
THE GREATEST SHOW ON EARTH, the marquee read, untouched.
And who would doubt the claim? It all seemed choreographed,
red curtains drawn on new illusions as we watched.
Coke bottles melted into miniature lakes and streams—
those bits of brightness that my mind will never lift.
The act forged into blackened slag. We couldn't look away.

III

A Cut Path

switches back up the grassy dome and loses itself
in unbroken fog. I apologize for the weather,
California promises so much. "I'm not hard to please,"
she tells me, losing breath as we climb
the clay path, hoof-packed and lined
with broad saucers of shit. And I believe her,
or just let it rest. A single way
ramifies up the hillside, each spur
dead-ending in cropped grass and thistle.
A small cluster of cows inspect us as we pass.
We latch the gate behind.
                          And when the fog burns off,
a thin strip of ocean marks the middle distance
from where we are, watching lizards
scatter in sudden sunlight. The cows stand frozen
in portrait below, casting their doubles down the slope.
For us, a bit of wishful thinking has made
this hill a mountain, and we are now descending.

Distraction Display

Some birds, to fend
against predators,
will fake a battered
or broken wing
to redirect
attention from
their young. If this
is evolution's
best guess, well,
it's not a bad one.
Just yesterday,
I saw a grackle
dragging a wing
like out-of-water
tackle, then rise
from a tuft of clover,
tracking with ripe
chokecherry eyes
as it flew up
and over me.
It lit in a maple
by a nest I'd failed,
at first, to notice—
a minor thing
to thank distraction
for, when it
came into focus.

The Stones of Avebury

"Tender-handed stroke a nettle . . ."

Jutting like ragged cuspids from the earth,
they're vestiges of purpose only guessed at.
Now mild-mannered sheep regard their height
with profound indifference, grinding clots of grass
in clockwise circles.
                Jet-lagged, far from home,
I nagged with endless questions: *Where? What year . . . ?*
And though the weather wasn't what you'd hoped,
we turned along the henge, knee-high in rape
and spellbound by unfathomable age.
As we drove off, the stones flattened to distance
framed in your mirrors. An archipelago
of bumps reminded me of how I'd grazed
a nettle, passingly. And learned a phrase.

Glass Animals

"Not bad," you say, then nod to hide the fact
we've wasted half the afternoon by stopping.
We could be getting drunk at Chapter House,
and anyway, you're right: The case is dusty,
the little cards are barely legible,
and all the jellyfish have snapped or cracked.
There's still some life left in the octopus!
It fans out like a mottled carriage dress.
"Yeah, that one's good," although two tentacles
have dropped their ballast from its palm-sized mass.
A shower starts to blur the windowpanes.
The ill-lit hall grows dim. Tall cases glow.
We hurry into jackets, tuck our chins,
and slant through slanting rain, with you ahead—
a visitor, but leading as you go.

Late Visit

Light crowds the room. A man
reclines on a hospital bed,
surrounded by his family.
Each plays the harder part.

The man speaks, occasionally,
about the weather, and drifts
on the soft swells of morphine,
concerned with knots and tides.

He thanks everyone for coming,
then studies the white lilies
with a look of concentration
and thanks everyone for coming.

The nurses no longer hurry.
He turns to tell his wife
of forty-five years, "Honey,
you're the prettiest lady

on this boat," and smiles, holding
the bedrail like a gunwale.
She blushes, hiding her ring.
And no one will correct him.

Fruit Flies

In crooked paths, they waft
through August, pinging from
fruit to fruit, *gang aft*

agley, then rest on plum
or Brandywine to lay
their careful schemes: in sum,

thousands of eggs per day.
They curse each coffee cup
to drink the cream, and pay

with life for that one taste.
But I, being a man,
have countless tries to waste

in winging rot to rot,
pursuing finer things.
The hands of others swat

me, rising up and up—
a driven little fly
bound for a coffee cup.

The Portrait Artist

They show up smelling like their Food Court lunch,
picking at teeth and smoothing lumps of hair.
"It's for a Christmas card," Mom says. "Are there,
like, props and things?" I point her to a bunch

of stuffed elves, candy canes, and plastic candles.
Three little girls! Mom's youngish and demure.
Her ruffled dress looks like a Douglas fir.
You'd think it were a bomb, the way she handles

the diapered one, face pinched, needing a change.
And where's Dad, anyway? That callow shit
took off, no doubt. These days, it's hitch and split.
Oh, well; there's one less body to arrange.

And that's the trick: It's how you ply the scene,
much more than shutter, flash, and aperture.
See, when I let them pose as they prefer—
legs crossed, eyes crossed, a plastic Nazarene

in each child's lap—the portrait falls apart.
I need the little ones just so, and smiling.
What, tears? I work their bellies like I'm dialing
a rotary phone. Their joy, like any art,

needs no more than a master's gentle coaxing.
(An eager hand works only half as well.)
Even the bullish brats who squirm like hell,
or stick a surly tongue out when their folks sing

"Old MacDonald," have such an easy time
with me. So, when the parents make things worse,
I wish we were alone—and could rehearse,
the child and I, a more convincing rhyme.

For Christ's sake, look how crudely Mom corrals
her girls, hands grasping. One's begun to cry.
Another lifts her skirt: A blotchy thigh
gives way to festive panties, which Mom fails

to hide, rushing her hand toward modesty.
She blushes as I glide her to her seat,
then place those little graces at her feet.
They rock and coo. Their focus turns to me

as I give all proportion to the frame,
then make the moment still, and permanent.
And, honestly, that's all I ever meant—
in other words, to make the wild eye tame.

The Omey Races

After a losing bet on SHES MY BABY,
we skirt cloud-doubling puddles through the hum
of chip van generators, then mount the slope
up the tidal island, where past a roofless church
and scattered cattle, a single stone road thins
to rut and furrow, crags and livid sea.
"Next stop, America—" my guide points west
and leans on a lichened wall, long obsolete.
The wind is from the west; and further west,
a woman is waking where I'd rather be.

It's pissing rain. But walking back, he stops
to catch his breath and stares down at the gorse,
shuffling his Wellies, straightening an unmoved scarf.
Down on the sand, gulls beak the formless scraps
of bread and meat. Tide rushes slowly in
while bookies pack their boards for other fools.
The island, never gone, will reappear
as seawater comes to break this land from that.
For now, a joining strand runs at our feet.
I might have passed, not knowing it was there.

Leap into the Void

Yves Klein, 1960

Not seen: the tarp that breaks his fall.
Instead, a cyclist totters unmolested
through middle distance, although soon
he'll face the street's inevitable T.

The sky's undifferentiated smear of gray
is the same redundant gray that greases
the crescent of his fender as he goes.
A sign declares itself illegibly.

Behind, a suited man leans on the crutch
of air that props him up, mid-leap.
                                    How long
he must have crept across the roof,
toes edging toward the coping where he'd catch

the unfamiliar and descendant view:
brick alternating light to dark like sediment,
downward to where a painter's tarp
luffed in the morning's subtle coming-to.

A certain risk plays mother to our love.
Wingless, he blunders through the stories
toward the billowed give of canvas—
which, in the photograph, has been removed.

The Well-Tempered Clavier

From another room, a phrase I've heard before
travels the hall to our kitchen
where I slice garlic cloves, cut basil to ribbons.
The piece is so familiar I can't quite place it.

A low sun baffles through the oaks.
She works that same section over
and over, swearing softly
at missed notes, dozens maybe,
until she makes it through the fugue.
The rasp of pages turning turns to quiet.

I've started crushing canned tomatoes
into a pot stood over a little flame,
watching their juices boil into a tart steam
when she begins again—one voice
repeating, almost, what the other says.

The Illusionist

There is an art, he knows, to breaking down
the architecture of the make-believe:
    He must rehearse
  the concentrated frown,
the stuffing of each trick back up his sleeve,
    the *fiat* in reverse.

An unacknowledged master of thin air,
he swallows cigarettes and turns up queens
      while shoppers arc
  across the city square.
As evening comes, the thinning sunlight leans
    against the cobbled dark.

Like popcorn faltering, the crowd's applause
slows to a stop. Now for the final act,
    he packs his cases
  latch by latch, and draws
the tangled skeins of fiction back to fact.
    Still, disbelieving faces

goad him on, and—wanting more—demand
a deeper look inside his repertoire.
    His levities
  are merely sleight of hand,
but appearances alone will fill a jar.
    So, coin-eyed, he agrees.

Lamplight startles night back into day,
although imperfectly—the way belief
   at times inheres
   in what's half-hid away.
He turns the dove back to a handkerchief—
   then, grinning, disappears.

IV

Big Hedge

Atherton's aging poster child
still owns a colonial with his younger wife;
his terrier still sniffs along the fence.
His kids have grown and gone; his gardener
works at Home Depot with the other ciphers
and still needs papers.

Eager for all
the near-invisibility
that makes for good community,
he lives behind a massive hedge, four-square
like a curtain wall
that keeps us here, him there.

There are no seasons:
Sweetgums blush, but roses bud
all winter long; new CEOs
hire newer workers. Houses never flood.
There's barely water to fill a garden hose.
God punishes, but has his reasons.

And now, as almost every night,
my wife and I are woken from a sleep
half-watchful, half-deep
when something, sometime before dawn,
triggers the neighbor's alarm, which floods the lawn
with prophylactic light.

Drawing the curtains back, I find
the hedge obscuring nearly two full stories;
a bit of lattice strung with morning glories
still pent for the night; a magnesium brightness in the eaves;
and clinging to the lime, a pack of rats that rattle waxy leaves,
groping for fruit, well-fed and mostly blind.

Woodpecker

i.

Mornings, we listened to the windows stutter
while a cartoon figure drummed the cedar shakes,
blurring its beak like the Singer in our basement.
"Turn that thing off," we joked. "Come in already."
We half expected the iconic laugh.
Like humor, it was good until it wasn't.
Shut up, shut up, shut up.
                              We couldn't sleep.
One night, while lightning strobed the whitecap lawn,
Dad wandered out in just his Jockeys, cursing
the whole of nature—birds, the weather, God—
but it was only wind that lashed the chimes.
He cut them from the birch, then came back in
and tossed their tangled pipes into the trash.

ii.

"You shouldn't park there."
                              "Sorry. I didn't know."
"You see that sign? They're tearing down the house."
"My wife and I just—"
                              "Any day now."
                                             "—moved
into the neighborhood."
                              "I see that. Welcome.
We'd all prefer it if you parked your car
in front of—how'd you manage, by the way?"

"We saw an ad."
                   "Not many renters here.
This is a *neighborhood*. You might tell Pam
it's probably illegal, having you . . .
And Christ, look at that yard. You'd think—"

"We're quiet, both of us."
                              "Good thing."
                                             "We won't
be having people—"
                   "Fine."
                              "I mean, I doubt
you'll know—"
                   "Just move the car."
                                             "—we're even here."

iii.

Winded, slick with sweat, my wife and I
finish our run, then round the hedge to where—

"What, don't you work?" he says, two fat thumbs tucked
into his back support.

                    "No more than you do."

It doesn't *quite* come out the way I mean.
My wife just waves hello.

                    "Hey, *you* look strong,"
he says, nodding my way. Three denimed men
confer in Spanish, sizing up the tub
they'll need to lug up two full flights of stairs.

"Well, strong enough."

                    "A hundred bucks an hour,"
I tell him, walking by, although I'd *like*
to help install the tub, then draw a bath
and make him—
                    "Honey?"
                         "Yeah."
                              "Let's go inside."

iv.

A slight rain ticks. And from the corner lot
the muffled rumbling of small-windowed trucks
sounds distant, like a war not quite in season.
They've scraped a house away. Bright metal claws
tear into new old ground, turning it over
like a crop.
        Distracted now, I part the slats
to check on progress, but I know we can't
see past our little yard. There, in the mud,
Pam's old dog lies serene, licking the suet
from a plastic package of Woodpecker Treat.
I step outside, smooth back his supple ears
and shush him, though he's silent, as if to say,
This isn't yours. This isn't even yours.

Apology

Come evening, he plucks zucchini blooms.

The shriveled braids of saffron petals
line the counter, where one by one

he peels them back, scoops their stamens,
and plunges them headlong into batter—

then eases a batch into rippling oil,
which smokes and sputters as blossoms bob.

Unraveling the largest flower—
green-veined, plump—he neatly undresses

a honey bee, aroused and confused
by sudden light in a stranger garden.

With a preparatory flick and hum,
the tuneless rattle of onion-skin wings,

it wobbles off in drunken loops
and taps against the windowpane.

The oil hisses and spits its tacks.
He stops to sip the breathing wine,

remembering lastly to level the glasses
drop for drop before she returns.

Cozy Cottages Swept Clean
by Winds from the Sea

She hauls the fragments up from memory:
a girl; Cape Cod; ramshackle fences built
from furring strips, half-lashed with bits of wire
and leading, like a hallway, to the sea.
She searches, finds the rhyme.

And soon her *cozy cottages swept clean*
travel the miles to Mendocino County,
and him, a squatter in a summer rental
in a pygmy forest. The tiny branches seem
older than possible.

He reads the line, looks out to spindrift smoothed
by hanging fog. The specter of a beach
appears while, in the loft, his coffee cools.
The redwood beams grow fragrant with the light.
Below, sea and more sea.

People are friendly and believe in God . . .
As lines return to her, she jots them down
and sends them, giddy in her recollection
of what goes on, for other people now.
Later, she writes with more:

Someday I'll see my love again, Cape Cod . . .
He's never been before, but pictures her:
a girl, barefoot, dragging her fingertips
along the slender fence posts, unaware
of what she's running for.

He adds in bathers, salt-gray cedar shakes,
and clumps of marram sprouting from the dunes.
A gust upturns a turquoise beach umbrella.
The waves replace themselves without his prompting.
Now all he does is watch.

    —for my mother

Jim and Mary

We never spoke too much of them:
"Nice folks," or sometimes, "Look at the way . . . "
Strict virtue makes a shrinking list
of what we'd like to say.

Well-dressed, sustained by average means,
they indulged themselves in modest doses.
For discipline, Jim kept the paths
of Eisenhower and Moses.

One day while cleaning, Mary reached
to brush a spider from the wall,
but a ruptured berry in her brain
made Mary faint and fall.

Then Mary seemed a child again,
and she could barely take her tea.
And all that once made Mary Mary
wandered off, permanently.

Jim begged for mercy, healing, prayer,
proof, theory, or Magnificat.
She tried to speak, but mostly Mary
sat and sat and sat.

They kept away. Though Mary liked
to see the sidewalk crocuses,
Jim turned the bolt. Nothing stays
or is what it promises.

So he took her where the train tracks run
like miles of zipper teeth through town,
out past the boarded paper mill
the Moreys had shut down.

They stood in sunlight like young lovers.
They felt the stirring April breeze.
They suffered the bitterness that came
from blooming Callerys.

The whole world was a reverdie.
The far light was a kind of beacon.
Jim held firm to Mary's hand
and felt the daylight weaken.

The 6:03 was punctual.
It trundled unerringly down the track.
Jim heard—did Mary?—the wheels that said,
get back, get back, get back.

Echo Lake

Hunkering underneath a shaggy fir,
he shifts when sunlight shifts its bit of shade
and eats a single almond every hour.
A fizzing galaxy of dark stars swarm
the matted, still-wet grass where he was sick.

"We're gonna laugh when we look back at this,"
he tells me. It's a good thing there's no mirror.
Now and again, he stumbles from the shade
to retch. I take his pulse and check for service,
but I know it's useless. "Such a perfect place,"
he says despite himself.
                            Out on the lake,
cliff swallows sketch the surface, then disappear
into the granite ridge that cuts the light
and tricks the distance into something near.

September 12, 1967

Staggered with news of wastage in Quảng Nam
and Woolworth's ads for nuts and chocolate stars,
a headline: *Youth Dies; Auto Hits Parked Cars*.
Gone at eighteen years old, he left my mom

an only child: *high rate of speed; car failed;*
out of control; a student at Paul Smith's . . .
The obit spans three meager finger-widths,
and yet it covers how the Ford fishtailed

around the curve, hit hard enough to buck
my uncle past the windshield's little knives,
then laid him roadside—where his form arrives
at my imagination's end. What luck

set down in ink, idle conjecture blurs:
I tap the brake or shift the cars—a game
that reconfigures how a man became
the date-stamped paperwork of coroners.

An accident, they said, though some blamed booze.
All I can say is plain from page 15
of Watertown's *Daily Times*: He's pressed between
a headline and an ad for dancing shoes.

Distracted by an Empty Cheetos Bag

after James Arthur

On a sunny afternoon in the best year
of my life, as palm trees cast stabs of shadow
on honeycomb brick, I watched an empty bag
of Cheetos billow with the wind and scrape
past my feet. No one else saw this, and so

it was all mine: a fine aluminum sail moving
graceful as a theorem. It was irrefutable.
My mental grocery list vanished, meaning
fennel might have been what I'd meant to buy,
likely as eggs or ground turkey.

    A Cheetos bag. A Cheetos bag. It skated off—
toward other trash, I guess. Instead of the store,
I went home, where I undressed, my good suit
in a pool of its own melting where it fell.
I sat on the couch in just my underwear

and watched the ticker tape of news till dark.
But the empty bag kept skating at my feet,
or my mind's feet. And as the president,
himself an alarming orange, dictated
my fears to me, I thought about fingers

still carrying that same faint glow long after
the last Cheeto vanished, its little crook
of mostly air digested now. Don't ask
me why, but these days I can't stop eating them,
letting the bright crumbs gather on my lips.

The Remedy

after a drawing by Watteau

She looks calmed by the nurse's hand,
which reaches for a sloping buttock while
the other readies a clyster syringe.

I stand plausibly between this drawing
and another—one with no nudity, no nipple
brushing the red-*crayon* duvet

on which a woman lies in half-repose,
waiting for that rush of warm water.
I swear she's almost smiling.

For nearly an hour, my wife has been lost
in a Flemish world of peasantry and the hunt.
But now I notice her returning, and when

she's just behind me, I ask what she thinks.
"I like it," she says. "I'm guessing you like
the colors? Or is it just her nice—?" A joke,

meaning the softness of that curve,
my attention for it. Of course, it's true,
but more than Watteau's willing figure,

I'm thinking of my own, on its side,
knees drawn up like a child napping.
And I'm thinking how the gown

slides down off my thigh, baring the full
nakedness of my back, like in a worry dream.
A nurse checks the propofol IV,

and the doctor asks if I'm alright
with being observed by an intern.
After I say okay, a woman enters —

white-coated, stunningly young. I'm thinking
of the gown's tiny red poppies, and how
they're suddenly absurd, she is so beautiful.

I'm thinking of that humid afternoon
my brother took an aluminum bat
to the face when Danny hit a home run

into the neighbor's lawn. Danny rounded
two makeshift bases before noticing the blood
that came in rills from my brother's nose.

He just sort of moaned, his look far-off.
I rounded the side of the house, leaving him
to bleed while I shook by the flower garden.

Later, I tore down all my plastic pennants
and fell asleep on the floor with the light on.
Summer ended that year in the middle of June.

"What is it?" my wife asks, squinting at the sketch.
And I tell her about how, when I was much younger,
I could sleep anywhere — under the copper beech,

or on the itchy red mat in my parents' foyer—
if I lay on one side and brought my knees up
the way kids do, not meaning to forget.

Acknowledgments

Grateful acknowledgment is due to the editors of the following publications, where many poems in this collection first appeared, sometimes in different versions:

American Arts Quarterly: "Apology"
The Common: "The Stones of Avebury" and "Waiting on Results"
The Hopkins Review: "Jim and Mary"
Literary Imagination: "September 12, 1967"
The Missouri Review: "In Flight" and "The Portrait Artist"
The New Criterion: "A Cut Path" and "Fruit Flies"
New Walk Magazine: "Titan Arum"
Parnassus: "The Vanishing Bird Cage"
Poetry: "The Magic Trick"
PN Review: "As Is," "Distraction Display," "Glass Animals," "Not the Song, but After," and "TO WHOM IT MAY CONCERN . . . "
Salmagundi: "Big Hedge," "Distracted by an Empty Cheetos Bag," and "The Remedy"
Southwest Review: "Rasmus Nielsen" and "Tiny Tina"
The Yale Review: "Echo Lake," "The Illusionist," "The No— Pond Hermit," "Petty Theft," and "Undark"

Acknowledgment is due for later appearances in *Poetry*, *The New York Times*, and *From the Finger Lakes: A Poetry Anthology*, as well as on *Poetry Daily*, E-Verse Radio, and National Public Radio.

"Undark" would not exist in its current form without Eleanor Swanson's "Radium Girls." "Rasmus Nielsen" would not exist at all without B. H. Fairchild's "Frieda Pushnik" or Stewart O'Nan's *The Circus Fire*.

My sincerest thanks to Cornell University for a place in their program; to Stanford University for the generous support of a Wallace Stegner Fellowship; and to the Poetry Foundation for a Ruth Lilly Fellowship.

I am indebted to the judges of The New Criterion Poetry Prize. To everyone who encouraged these poems, my deepest gratitude.

And to Anne-Marie, all my days.